IN THE FACES OF MEN AND WOMEN I SEE GOD

Portraits And Other Images From India

"Why should I wish to see God better than this day? I see something of God each hour of the twenty-four, and each moment then. In the faces of men and women I see God, and in my own face in the glass. I find letters dropped in the street, and every one is signed by God's name, And I leave them where they are, for I know that whereso'er I go others will punctually come forever and forever."

— Walt Whitman
Song Of Myself

Acknowledgements

There are two people without whom this book would not be possible.

My wife, Mary Ann, and I have travelled together in India several times. On many other occasions, though, I've taken lengthy trips alone, and without her support I would not have had the time or opportunity to collect the photos that are in this book.
Thank you many, many times over for your support, and for taking such good care of business while I'm gone!

Digambar Samal is driver, guide and companion without peer. Since 1996 he has taken us to places which I would never have been able to visit on my own.

Samal's outgoing and engaging personality has allowed us to connect with people throughout India; from the largest cities to the most remote countryside.

Thank you for all you have done already and also for all those trips we have yet to take!

INDIA
State and Union Territories

Introduction

I first visited India in 1973. Mary Ann and I had spent the prior year in Afghanistan, and the last few weeks in Ceylon, (presently Sri Lanka), so we were not unfamiliar with Central and South Asia. Nothing, however, had prepared us for the pandemonium which broke loose as we stepped from the airport terminal building into the steamy Madras evening.

Apparently every rickshaw and taxi driver, porter, hotel tout, banana hawker and curiosity seeker in town had shown up expecting to somehow benefit from our arrival. It took an almost violent effort to break through the ranks of shouting, gesticulating and grasping Indians, just to find a cab and flee to a downtown hotel.

It wasn't love at first sight, with India. We were on a Peace Corps budget, which meant lots of busses, third-class trains and time spent ferreting out the cheaper hotels. It was, granted, an excellent way to be immersed in the local culture, but this sensory assault often felt overwhelming and left us longing for the quiet of our Afghan village.

On our way home in 1974, we traveled overland through India again, out of the necessity of getting to Nepal cheaply. Many of the foreigners we met in Katmandu had been to India, for varying lengths of time. No one was neutral about their experience! On one extreme was the young Brit who said, "On my first day there, somebody nicked me wallet and then one of those bloody sacred cows gored me in me privates. I left the next day, and I'm never goin' back!" Opposing this view was the 32 year old man who had arrived in 1966, for a three week visit, and who was still there, 8 years later. He said that he had never felt such peace as during his time in India. It's a land of contradiction, that's for certain.

We arrived back in the U.S.A. with no intention of returning to India, at least not anytime soon. But, somehow, the inexplicable lure of the place had me planning another, longer trip, and in 1976 we set off again, for a four month stay. We criss-crossed the country and accumulated a set of remarkable experiences. Now, though, it seemed clear that we really were finished with India, possibly forever. And, for the next 20 years it appeared that way, although I did make a few very brief stops on the way to somewhere else.

Then in 1996, I came across a program calling for volunteers to assist in a wolf-habitat research program in Gujarat. Finding that program seemed like rainfall to a dormant seed. Combined with an affection for wolves, it was the perfect opportunity for a return to India. On this trip I wanted to do some serious photography; going and stopping when and where I wished, so I decided to hire a car and driver for the several weeks of travel before and after the project.

I found my driver—rather, he found me, in a hotel parking lot in Bhubaneshwar. Since that serendipitous moment, Samal and I have journeyed together five more times, most recently in 2005, covering just about every region of the country.

India has changed certainly, since 1973. The population is now over a billion, the roads are crowded with cars of the growing middle-class, satellite dishes give remote villages access to previously unseen wonders like Bollywood movies and CNN, and there are many other evidences of a more prosperous and open economy.

Somehow, though, the past hangs on. Each trip that I see the nomads with their flocks of sheep, children riding on top of the camels, and lambs in the saddlebags, I think it will be for the last time; yet so far it has not been. The contrasts between urban and rural, and rich and poor, are just as distinct as ever, perhaps more so. The disorderly carrying on of life, out in plain view, spiced with pungent smells, lurid colors, chaotic markets, ear-splitting movie music and wandering cows, has yet to be swept out with the tides of "progress." India is no Singapore and thank God for that.

There is something else that has not changed either; those moments of, "Please Lord, get me out of here. I promise to never come back!" Being over-stimulated, over-heated, over-dusted, and over-whelmed are all still part of the experience. Each of my prior three trips, in fact, has been declared to be the last one ever. But, as the philosopher Pascal once said, "The heart has its reasons, which reason knows nothing of." So I continue to return.

Having said all that, this book isn't really about India the country. It's about people, mostly, who happen to live there. Nowhere on earth, I think, can one experience so much pure, unsanitized, unself-conscious humanness as in India.

The definition of evoke is, "to recreate an emotion through the experience of the memory and imagination." I hope that, once removed though they are, these images still retain the evocative power of the original subjects.

Larry Heeren

Assam 2001

9

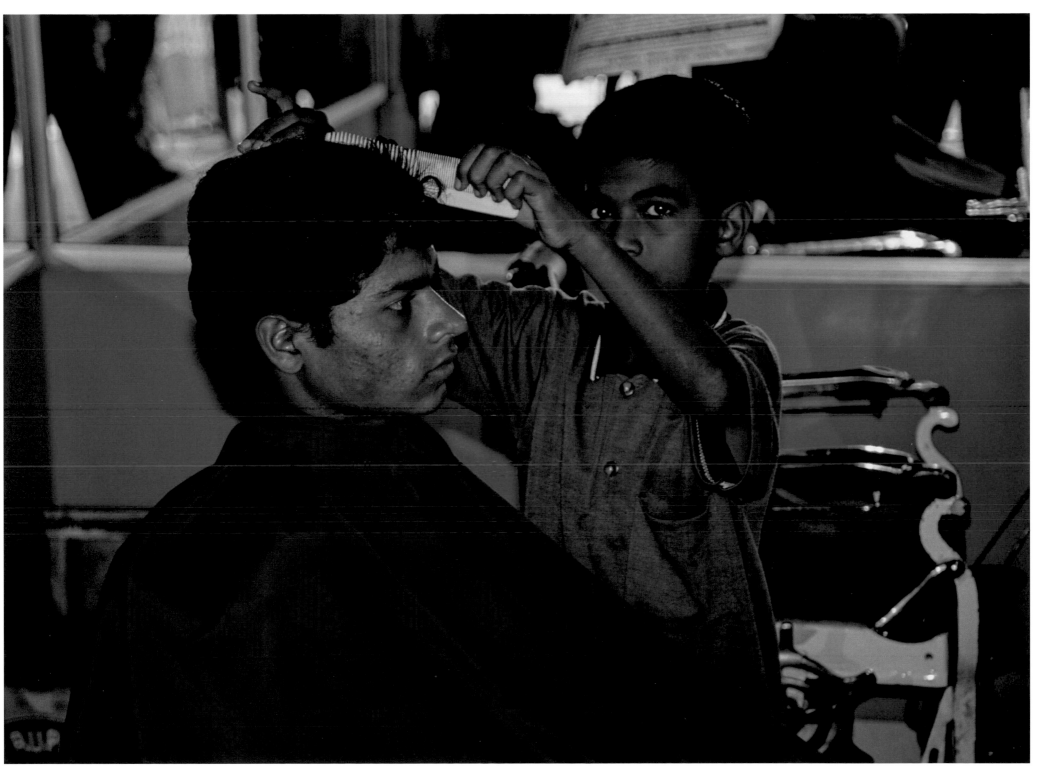

"He is a very clever boy, but I am not allowing him to use the razor yet!"
   Father of town's youngest barber

Saputara, Gujarat 2005

Orissa 2004

Jaisalmer, Rajasthan   1999

Motherless puppy raised by monkey.

Patna, Bihar 1999

Karnataka 2004

Tales of Hanuman

Hanuman is the red-faced monkey warrior of Hindu myth, child of a nymph and the Wind God.

According to the Ramayana, the ancient Sanskrit epic named for Prince Rama, the demon king Ravana abducted Rama's wife, Sita. Ravana took Sita across the ocean from India and imprisoned her in Lanka (the present day Sri Lanka).

Rama needed help and the loyal Hanuman obliged by leaping to Lanka in a single bound. Once there the wily monkey discovered Sita's whereabouts, but was captured in the process and dragged before the demon Ravana.

"Questioned by Ravana's minister, Hanuman answered that he was indeed a monkey, come to Lanka as Rama's envoy to accomplish his commands and to behold Ravana; and he told the story of Rama up till then, and gave Ravana sound advice; to save his life by surrendering Sita. Ravana was furious and would have Hanuman slain, but the counselors reminded him that the punishment of death could not justly be inflicted upon one who named himself an envoy. Then Ravana cast about for a fitting penalty, and bethought him to set Hanuman's tail afire. Then the rakshasas (demons) bound the monkey's tail with cotton soaked in oil and set it all ablaze. But the heroic monkey cherished a secret plan; he suffered the rakshasas to lead him about Lanka that he might the better learn its ways and strength. Then word was taken to Sita that that monkey with whom she conversed was led about the streets of Lanka and proclaimed a spy, and that his tail was burning. Thereat she grieved, and praying to the Fire, she said: "As I have been faithful to my lord, do thou be cool to Hanuman!" The Fire flamed up in answer to her prayer, and at that very moment Hanuman's sire, the Wind God, blew cool between the flame and Hanuman. Perceiving that the fire still burnt, but that his tail was icy-cold, Hanuman thought that it was for Rama's sake and Sita's and his sire's that the heat was chilled, and he snapped his bonds and sprang into the sky, huge as a mountain, and rushed to and fro in Lanka, burning the palaces and all their treasures. And when he had burnt half Lanka to the ground and slaughtered many a rakshasa, Hanuman quenched his tail in the sea."

As a result of Hanuman's heroism, Rama returned to Lanka with massive force, defeated Ravana, and rescued Sita.

Thus, monkeys are revered by most and considered sacred by many in Hindu India.

Andhra Pradesh   1998

Bikaner, Rajasthan   2005

Ganges River, Bihar   1999

Pushkar, Rajasthan   1976

Calcutta 1999

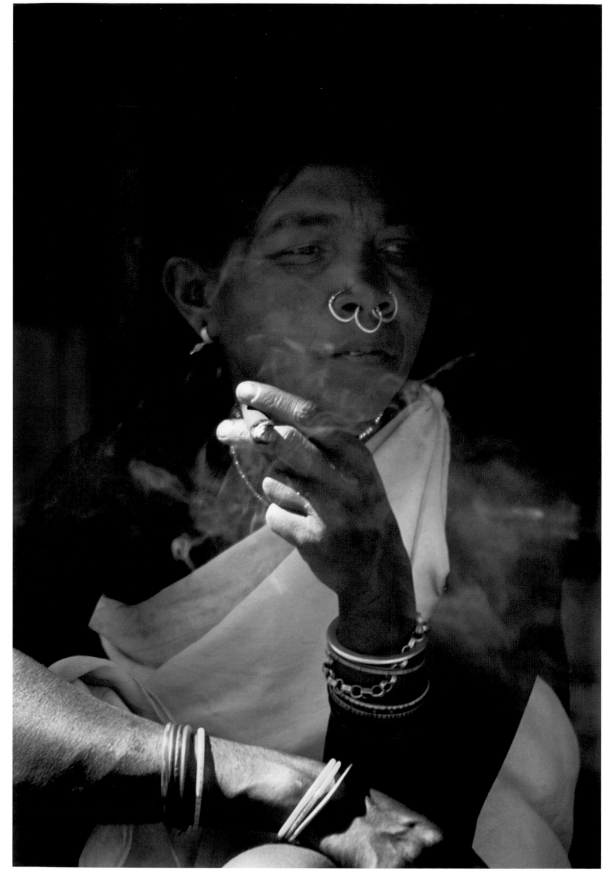

Orissa 2004

Gujarat   2005

23

Gujarat 2005

24

Got milk?

Gujarat   2005

Calcutta 1997

Calcutta 1997

Calcutta 1997

Calcutta 2004

Tamil Nadu   2004

Jhunjunun, Rajasthan 2005

Married 43 years

Jodhpur, Rajasthan   2005

Calcutta 1997

Calcutta   1997

Calcutta 1999

Assam   1999

Brahmaputra River, Assam   1999

Hugli River, Calcutta   1976

Orissa 1996

Karnataka   2004

Tamil Nadu   2004

Rajasthan 2005

Sheep Trick

There are some tribes in Gujarat, especially up near the Pakistan border, whose occupation is snake handling. This involves catching them, training them, displaying them at home and on the road, and, nowadays, often selling the venom for medical purposes. These folk are in high demand during the monsoon, when the torrential rains flush all sorts of creatures out of their usually dry homes.

Many in the tribe are also skilled magicians. I have seen several groups of these men, in Gujarat and Rajasthan, carrying small sacks of snakes and a few coins or pebbles as props for their magic show.

In Rajasthan recently, Samal and I pulled up at a roadside shop for tea and to stretch. A cluster of red-turbaned fellows hunkered nearby on the dusty ground, in the shade of a few scrawny mesquite trees. Their walking sticks and shoulder bags indicated that they were on some sort of walkabout. The ever gregarious Samal quickly struck up a conversation and discovered that they were indeed snake handlers/ magicians from Gujarat. They were spending some of the off season wandering, on foot, around the region, taking in the sights and doing the occasional show.

One of them beckoned me over and proceeded to pull a rupee coin out of my ear, and then turn the coin into a pebble. After a few more such tricks I was almost convinced that he was really a sorcerer, not just a sleight-of-hand artist. Samal certainly thought so. When one of the men took him aside and spoke to him, I saw Samal flinch. The magician had apparently hinted that he might turn Samal into a sheep! This did not come to pass, and after buying a round of tea for the house, we took our leave.

As we drove off, I asked Samal if he had been afraid of becoming a sheep. He said that, no, this magician wasn't strong enough to turn anyone into anything.

"But do you remember that tantric wizard we met in Assam? Now he was a powerful man, and if he wanted, he could turn both of us into sheep!"

Gujarat   1996

Gujarat 1998

Arunachal Pradesh   2001

47

Maharashtra 2005

Shekawati, Rajasthan 2005

51

Gujarat 2005

Bhavnagar, Gujarat   2005

Gujarat 1996

Maharashtra 2005

Orissa 2004

Haryana 2005

Uttar Pradesh   1999

"Who Tooks Lawrence?"

Samal and I left Patna early one October morning. On our way out of town we stopped for bananas, the perfect road food in India. Bananas are cheap, sanitary, good for you, and cows love to eat the peels.

Samal went off to the market, while I remained in the back seat. But, as he was slow in returning and I was thirsty , I wandered over to a tea stall and had a cup. After a brief question and answer session with the locals, I settled up and turned back to where I'd left the car.

To my dismay, and the crowd's amusement, I was just in time to see the white Ambassador pull onto the highway, Samal staring intently ahead, the tail lights receding into the distance.

I wasn't especially concerned. I estimated maybe 10 minutes for Samal to discover his error and be back.

Half an hour later, a cheer went up from the fair-sized gathering, and a voice from the rear called out, "Sir, your driver is now in sight!"

As I got into the car Samal said, "I am very glad to see you. Many dangerous people live here."

Three years later Samal, my friend Philip and I were sitting in a very seedy bar, inappropriately named the Casa Luxo, in the former Portuguese colony of Diu. Among Diu's many attractions is the absence of tax on alcohol. Therefore, a large Taj beer costing 120 rupees in neighboring Gujarat is a mere 30 rupees in Diu. Beer drunk, tongue loosened, Samal recalled the time he had left Lawrence behind in Bihar. "Let me tell you about that!"

"That morning I bought bananas and quickly got back into the car. I wanted to leave and get away from Bihar, due to that, as you know, Bihar is full of criminals.

The road is very crowded so I am paying attention straight in front of me as I drive. Finally, after a while I start to talk to you but I don't hear your voice. I think maybe you are asleep, but then I also know that you never sleep in the car. I talk some more but still you do not answer so I look into my mirror and ….

'MY GOD! WHERE IS LAWRENCE? WHO TOOKS LAWRENCE?' My whole body is vibrating! There are so many bandits and goondas here that I am afraid someone has taken you away. Of course now I turn around and drive back like a crazy man. All I can think about is who tooks Lawrence and I am praying to God that I find you when I get back to that place."

We laugh about it now, but according to Samal, his wife still reminds him of the time he left his customer behind. "Digambar," she asks, "How could you lose such a big man as Lawrence?"

Landlord with protection

Bihar 1999

Arunachal Pradesh   2001

Madhya Pradesh   1998

West Bengal   1999

Andhra Pradesh   1998

Madhya Pradesh   1998

Bombay   2005

Patna, Bihar   1999

Bombay   2005

Orissa 1998

Chhattisgarh 2004

Jodhpur, Rajasthan   2005

73

Bangalore, Karnataka   1976

Bengalis celebrate Durga Puja.

Somnath, Gujarat   2005

Gujarat 2005

76

Orissa 1996

Maharashtra 2005

Uttar Pradesh 1999

Pondicherry 2004

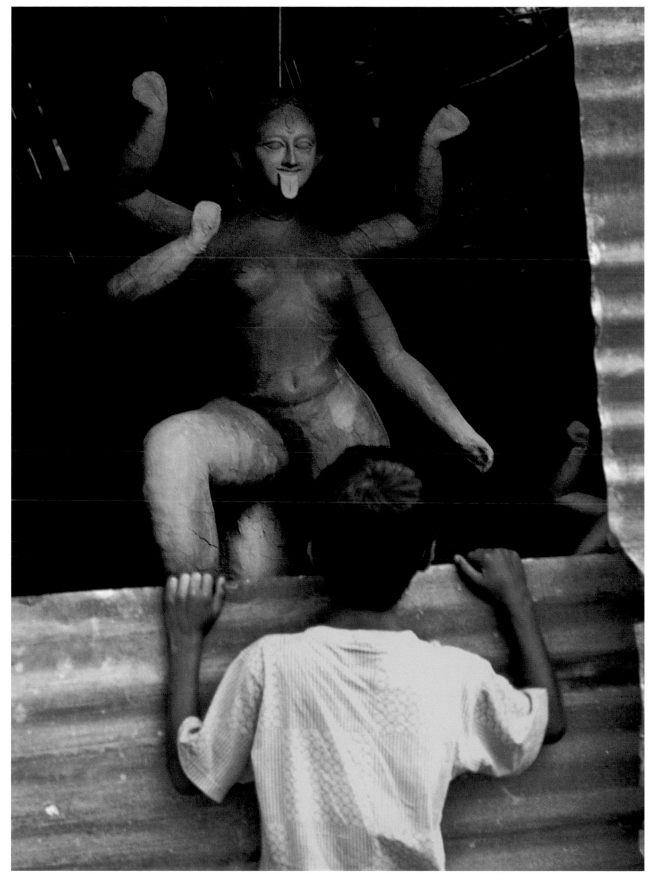

Assam 1999

Lohargar, Rajasthan 2005

Gujarat 1996

Gujarat   2005

Samal's Popsicles

"WHERE IS THE MORON WHO GAVE YOU THOSE POPSICLES??"

It was probably the girls' giggling that had alerted the proprietor. We saw him fly out of house, find the source of such merriment, and bellow his outrage. As his gaze fell upon Samal and me, he realized that he had made a mistake; there were actually two morons.

We had stopped at this place in Karnataka, drawn by endless piles of red chilies and chattering girls. During the harvest, young girls like these are recruited from villages in neighboring Andhra Pradesh to do the hard work of picking and then sorting the chilies.

As we watched, and Samal answered the girls' questions about which planet his white companion might be from, we heard the ring of a bicycle bell. We took no notice until the rider, a lad of 10 or 11 years, stopped at the farm entrance and announced that he had cold ices, very cheap, in the little metal box strapped on the back of his bike.

Samal is a generous man. He thought that after a day in the blistering heat and dusty fields the girls would appreciate something cold and wet. So he bought twelve popsicles, the boy's total inventory, and gave them out, one to each of the eleven girls, eating the twelfth himself.

The boss's wrath, out of politeness to me, was directed only at Samal. His wrath, however, was not for the reason we had assumed; that the girls should be working, not eating. No! He wondered aloud how anyone could be so stupid as to give them something ice-cold to eat in the middle of a scorching hot day. It is well known, says he, that such eating causes imminent and possibly grave illness, and what did we have to say about that! I, of course, had nothing to say, but Samal begged forgiveness for the ignorance of the two well-meaning strangers, and did the boss know that the man from America standing in front of him was very knowledgeable about health issues, practically a doctor in fact, and the latest information was that cold food and drink was good for people in the hot weather, and, by the way what is the price for a kilo of local chilies, etc. etc.

Samal's schmoozing seemed to have a calming effect, and next we knew we were seated on the porch in conversation with the now affable man and his wife. Later, in the car, I praised Samal's ability to diffuse our host's irritation, but he would take little credit for that. What had in fact happened, he said, was that he had heard the owner's wife's voice rise above the hubbub demanding in no uncertain terms that her husband cease browbeating the visitors and immediately invite them in for tea and biscuits!

Karnataka 2005

Orissa 1996

Bhubaneshwar, Orissa   1998

Priest leads harvest procession.

Ladakh, Jammu and Kashmir   1976

Orissa 1996

Maharashtra 2005

Tamil Nadu   2004

Karnataka 1998

Hassan weaves cloth.

Malgaon, Maharashtra   2005

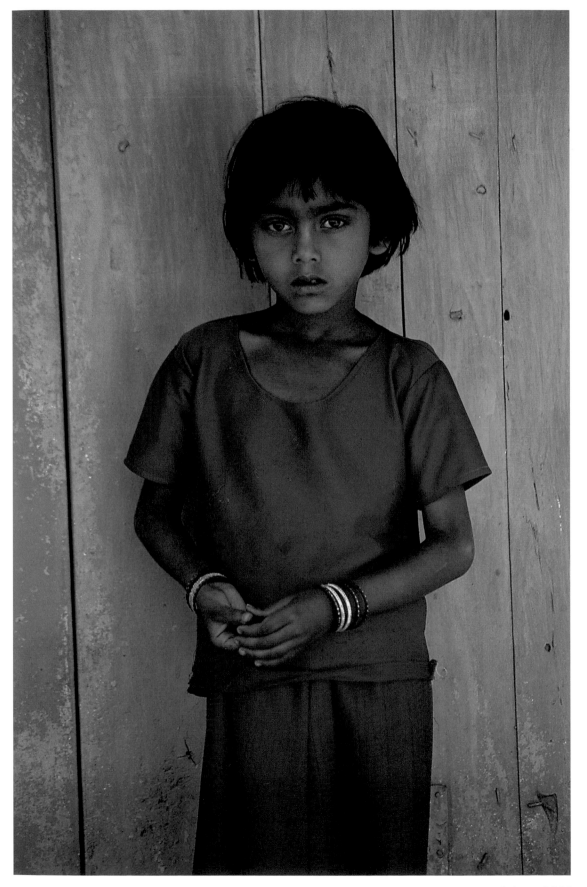

Orissa   2004

Orissa 2004

Tea   _Assam 2001_

Rice

Andhra Pradesh 1998

Uttar Pradesh   1999

Rajasthan 2005

Gujarat 2005

Arunachal Pradesh 2001

Orissa 1999

Chhattisgarh 2004

Cockfight bets   *Chhattisgarh   2004*

Ladakh, Jammu and Kashmir   1976

Leh, Ladakh 1976

Kutch, Gujarat 1998

113

Jantar Mantar

Delhi   1976

Orissa 1999

115

Rajasthan 1999

Pork and Bees In Nagaland

The far Northeast doesn't seem at all like the rest of India. In Arunachal Pradesh and Nagaland especially, just about everything is different; language, culture, religion, geography, and eating habits.

The food of India is wonderful, but if it's considered exotic that is primarily because of the spicing. The ingredients consist mostly of vegetables, grains, legumes, pulses and lesser amounts of lamb, chicken, and fish or other seafood. Fruit, nuts, and dairy products pretty much round out the list. The seemingly infinite variety and combinations of these ingredients, plus the skillful use of spices, make Indian cuisine one of the most interesting in the world.

Nagaland is more like Burma, with which it shares a long border, than India. A partial list of foods for sale in the market would include squirrels, monkeys, snakes, dogs, songbirds, spiders, and grubs. In addition to these delicacies, wild boar and domestic pig are common in the Naga diet.

There are many varieties of grubs to be had, from the tough to tender, cheap to expensive. One of the most coveted is the large, white larvae of a very angry looking jungle bee. We once observed an intact nest of these beauties which had been ripped from a tree and brought to market.

When our Naga guide offered to cook us a special Naga meal, Philip and I readily accepted (even as Samal respectfully declined). The meal began with bee larvae and ended with pig.

Since then, the short answer to, "What did you eat in Nagaland?", has been, ***"Pork and Bees!"***

Nagaland 2001

Jodhpur, Rajasthan 2005

Rajpipla, Gujarat   2005

Assam 1999

Tamil Nadu   2004

Sonepur, Bihar   2001

Rekha helps her blind Grandmother.

Ajanta, Maharashtra   2005

Saputara, Gujarat   2005

"Welcome to Bihar!"

One of the joys of travel in India is the number of celebrations, fairs, and festivals that one chances upon, simply by being in the right place at the right time.

On a late afternoon, driving in northern Bihar, we noticed groups of mostly women, shockingly bright even by Indian standards, baskets on head, moving along the road toward the nearest body of water. Curious, Samal made inquiries, and was told that this was the final day of a uniquely Bihari festival, called Chhath, dedicated to Surya, the sun god.

On this final day, devotees bring their offerings of food to water's edge, wade in and give prayer to Surya. As darkness descends, they move back away from the water, singing hymns, twinkling like so many fireflies from the light of the oil lamp each carries.

When we encountered an exceptionally large gathering not long before dusk, we sprang from the car and plunged into the crowd, attempting to get some photos while we still had a bit of light.

Samal, Philip and I each headed off in different directions, and after a few minutes I found myself being escorted, by a pair of teen-age boys, up into a sort of stage area overlooking the magnificent scene. The stage was populated with what appeared to be the cream of local society, and having let out that I was from America, I was given preferred seating as would befit some foreign dignitary.

A P.A. system had been set-up and a master of ceremonies of sorts was talking non-stop to the throng below. What exactly he was saying I wasn't sure, but I did begin to notice that the word America was peppering his speech, accompanied by frequent pointing in my direction.

Even as I sensed what was coming, my wits failed me, and when he thrust the microphone into my hand and exhorted me to address the crowd, all I could think to do was to shout out, ***"Welcome to Bihar!"*** The crowd energetically applauded its approval!

Usually I'm happy to find people who can understand English, but this evening I was glad almost no-one did.

Chhath

Bihar   1999

Rajasthan 1999

Orissa 1998

Gujarat 1996

Bonda girls serve home brew.

Orissa 1996

Diu 2005

Orissa 2004

Gujarat   2005

Dancing for Durga Puja

Rajpipla, Gujarat   2005

Apa Tani Woman   *Arunachal Pradesh   2001*

Hyderabad, Andhra Pradesh 1998

The Honored Guest

One night we came to a restaurant around dinner time. It was like hundreds of restaurants at which we've eaten throughout India. That is to say that it was loud, hot, almost frantically busy. Underage boys scuttled about, delivering food, or vaguely wiping down tables with oily black rags. Bits of potato, rice, bread, or maybe chicken or fish bones, littered the floor. The food would be excellent and cheap. I was the only non-Indian present; probably the first ever to eat here.

Before I sat, an older waiter dusted off my chair. Then he fled to the kitchen, reappearing with a small vase of plastic flowers and a placemat, laid in front of me. My first reaction, upon seeing the food-flecked mat and the flowers coated with dust and grease, was to demand their removal. But I didn't. I looked around and saw that no-one else was getting his chair dusted: no-one else got a placemat or a bouquet.

The waiter was standing by, beaming; genuinely happy to have given an extra welcome and special touch to the meal of a foreign guest. I felt both ashamed and relieved— ashamed for my initial feeling and relieved that I had not acted upon it. I also felt very much honored.

How often, I wonder, are we oblivious to such gestures?

Calcutta 1999

Sonepur, Bihar   2001

Maharashtra 2005

Puri, Orissa   1996

Somnath, Gujarat   2005

Haryana 2005

148

Jodhpur, Rajasthan   2005

Rajasthan 2005

Hunger strike

Hyderabad, Andhra Pradesh   1999

Pushkar, Rajasthan 1976

Rajasthan 2005

Calcutta 1999

Penis Envy By The Ganges

I was walking down the bathing ghats in Hardwar, along the Ganges river, when a holy-man, sitting cross-legged, reading from a prayer book, motioned me over. As I approached, he motioned once again, indicating that I should sit down next to him. He continued reading prayers for quite some time, and I, imagining this to last for hours, got up to leave. Still reading the prayers, he vigorously indicated that I should remain, pointed to the clock tower across the river, and held up four fingers. I took this to mean that at 4:00 something would happen, so I waited. Indeed, as the bell rang four he closed the books and exclaimed in the King's English, "Now I can talk!"

He professed to be a yogi, of age 68. I would have put him at 50 maximum. He said it was the diet of milk, cheese, and fruit that kept him so youthful. He had become fluent in English in Calcutta, working in the book business. But now it was time to retire to the meditative life on the banks of the most holy river in India, the Ganges.

I wanted to photograph him, but he was reluctant and wanted to know why. I said that I wished to remember him and our encounter. He replied to never mind the photograph, but he would tell me some things that I would remember forever. So he talked about being a yogi.

"First, to be a yogi, you must be able to touch your nose with your tongue." This he did easily.

"Then you must be able to cleanse the body inside by putting a handkerchief in one side of your nose and pulling it out the other. Also, you must be able to swallow a three-foot long rag, clean the stomach, and then retrieve the rag."

He insisted that these were simple tasks that the most novice of yogis could perform. Now, he said, there were much more difficult exercises, the accomplishment of which would make one an exalted yogi.

These exercises consisted of taking in, through the penis, various liquids of increasing viscosity. They were in order of difficulty; water, milk, clarified butter (ghee), honey, and finally mercury.

"I, myself, have done water, and I have seen many do milk and ghee. I have also heard of someone locally who is successful with honey. Neither I, nor anyone I know, thinks it is really possible with mercury, for a mortal human. It is said that if you can intake mercury up your penis you will also be able to walk on water!"

Since I can't even manage the first task of being a yogi, I have given up any thoughts of moving up to the next levels. After thirty years, though, I have not forgotten him; he was right about that!

Ganges River in flood

Bihar 1999

Gujarat   2005

Rajasthan 2005

Rajasthan 2001

This Book is Dedicated To

**Sir Harry Paget Flashman
Brigadier-General V.C.
K.C.B., K.C.I.E.
1822-1915**

Additional Inspiration By

**George MacDonald Fraser
Robert Frost
T.E. Lawrence
David Lean
James Michener
Eric Newby
Wilfred Thesiger**

Special Thanks To

Philip Amdal

Friend, fellow photographer and great travelling companion.
Here's to many more journeys!

About the photographs

All photos were taken by the author, unless otherwise noted.

Where: India
When: 1976-2005
Cameras: Nikon F, Canon Elan SLR
Film: Fujichrome Provia primarily, some Kodachrome

The slides were digitally scanned with a Nikon Coolscan 5000 scanner. Using Adobe Photoshop, the images were then cropped, cleaned and color corrected for printing and publication.

Text translator: Jessica Morgan
Technical wizard: Robert Jordan
Printed in Korea by Amica Inc.,

Jagganath Publishing

1955 Sunset Avenue Southwest

Seattle, Washington 98116

ISBN-10 0-9789411-0-1

ISBN-13 978-0-9789411-0-9

Library of Congress control number: 2006933885